Table of Contents

Nurse Sharks

Nurse sharks live in the Atlantic and Pacific Oceans. They like warm, **shallow** waters. They are often found near coral reefs.

5

Nurse sharks are very big. They can grow up to 10 feet (3 m) long.

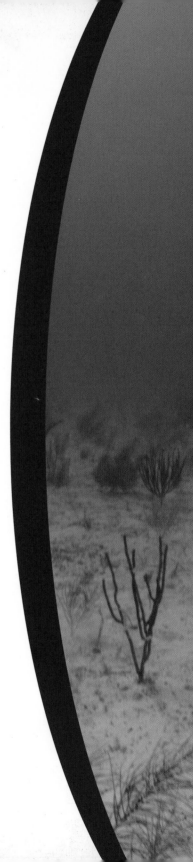

Nurse sharks are gray and

brown. Some have dark spots.

9

Nurse sharks have strong jaws.

They have tiny, sharp teeth.

11

Nurse sharks have two **barbels**. They are like whiskers. They are used to feel for **prey**.

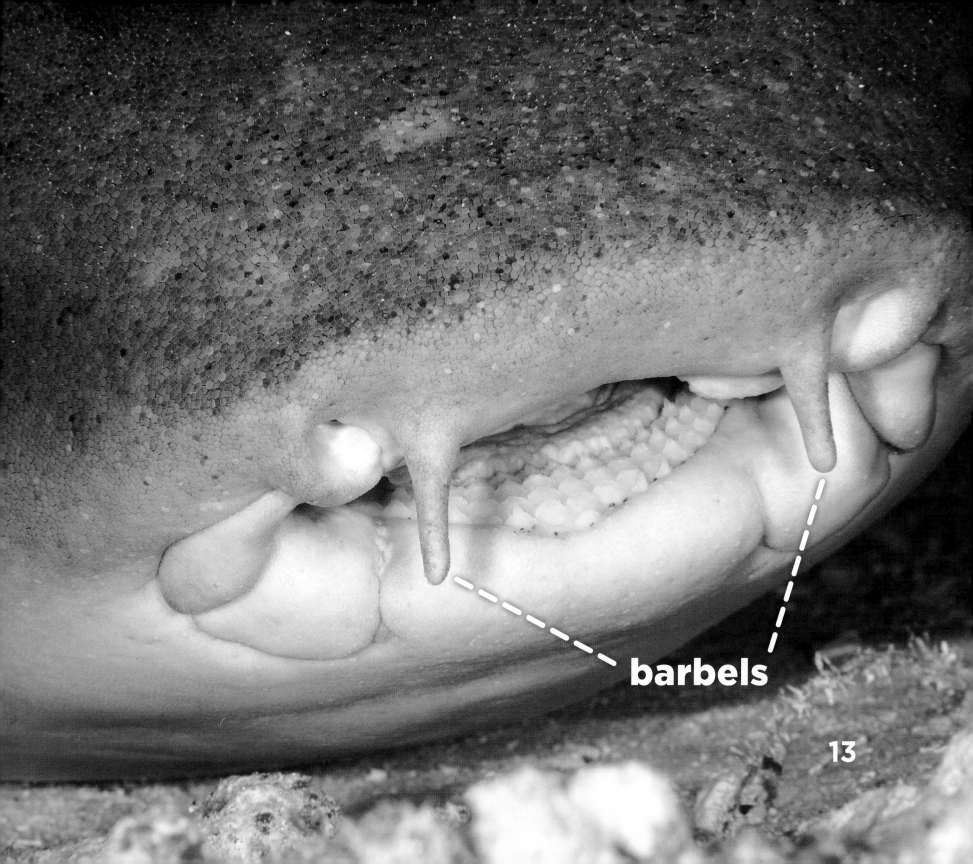

barbels

13

Nurse sharks rest during the day. They can be found clumped together.

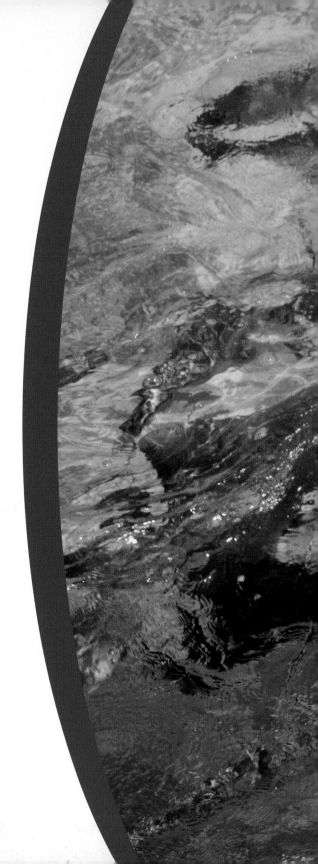

15

Food & Hunting

Nurse sharks hunt mostly at night. They move slowly along the ocean floor. Their **barbels** locate **prey**. The sharks lunge at the prey and suck it into their mouths.

16

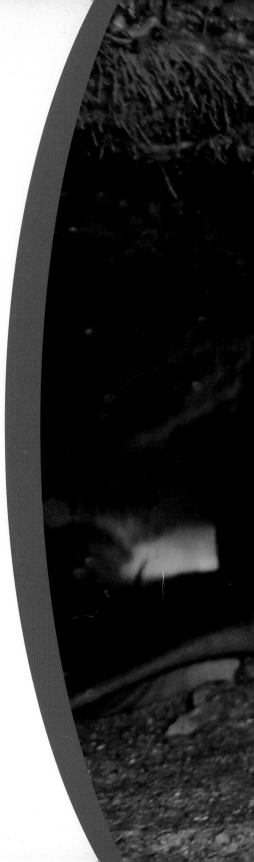

Nurse sharks eat lots of shellfish. But their favorite foods include squid and fish.

Baby Nurse Sharks

Baby sharks are called pups. Nurse sharks give birth to 20 to 30 pups. Mothers leave their pups right after birth.

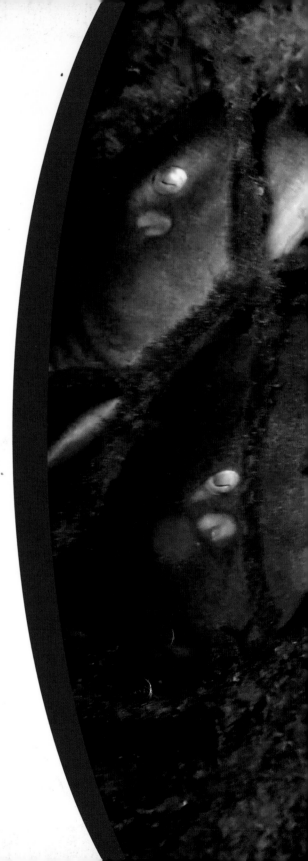

21

More Facts

- On average, adult females are longer and heavier than males.

- Nurse sharks have pups every other year.

- Pups are 11 to 12 inches (28 to 30 cm) at birth. Some will grow to be 10 feet long (3 m). But most grow to be around 7.5 feet (2.3 m) long.

Glossary

barbel – the whisker-like skin that grows from the snouts of sharks and other fish. It helps them feel for prey.

prey – an animal that is hunted and killed for food.

shallow – not deep.

Index

abdokids.com

Use this code to log on to abdokids.com and access crafts, games, videos, and more!

Abdo Kids Code:
SNK1538